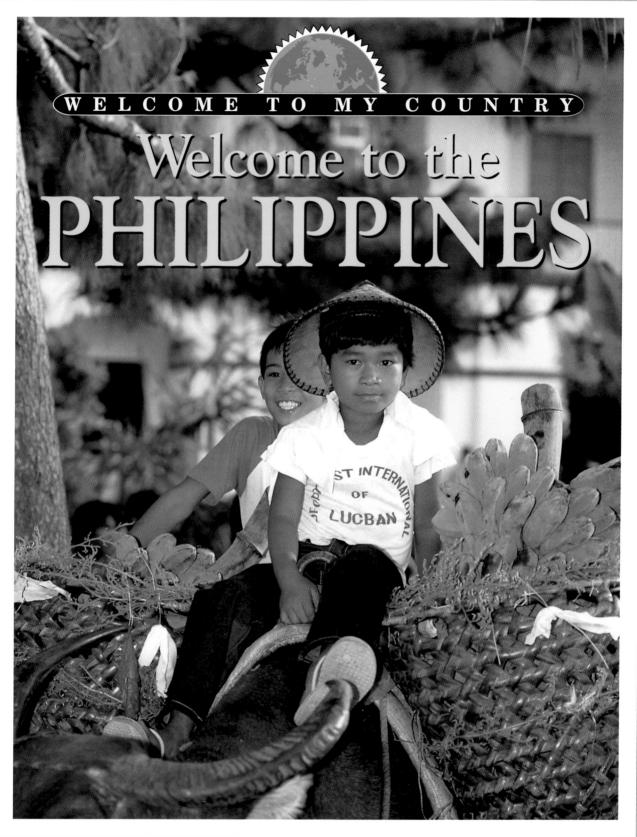

WELCOME TO MY COUNTRY

Welcome to the
PHILIPPINES

Gareth Stevens Publishing
A WORLD ALMANAC EDUCATION GROUP COMPANY

Written by
JO WYNADEN/JOAQUIN L. GONZALEZ III

Edited in USA by
ALAN WACHTEL

Designed by
JAILANI BASARI

Picture research by
SUSAN JANE MANUEL

First published in North America in 2002 by
Gareth Stevens Publishing
A World Almanac Education Group Company
330 West Olive Street, Suite 100
Milwaukee, WI 53212 USA

Please visit our web site at:
www.garethstevens.com
For a free color catalog describing
Gareth Stevens' list of high-quality books
and multimedia programs, call
1-800-542-2595 (USA) or
1-800-461-9120 (CANADA).
Gareth Stevens Publishing's
Fax: (414) 332-3567.

© **TIMES MEDIA PRIVATE LIMITED 2002**
Originated and designed by
Times Editions
An imprint of Times Media Private Limited
A member of the Times Publishing Group
Times Centre, 1 New Industrial Road
Singapore 536196
http://www.timesone.com.sg/te

Library of Congress Cataloging-in-Publication Data
Wynaden, Jo.
Welcome to the Philippines / Jo Wynaden and
Joaquin L. Gonzalez III.
p. cm. — (Welcome to my country)
Includes bibliographical references and index.
Summary: An overview of the Philippines that discusses the country's
geography, history, economy, people, and culture.
ISBN 0-8368-2534-9 (lib. bdg.)
1. Philippines—Juvenile literature. [1. Philippines.] I. Gonzalez,
Joaquin L. (Joaquin Lucero) II. Title. III. Series.
DS655.W96   2002
959.9—dc21   2001040623

Printed in Malaysia

1 2 3 4 5 6 7 8 9 06 05 04 03 02

PICTURE CREDITS
Agence de Presse ANA: 5 (top), 9 (bottom),
   18 (top)
Archive Photos: 5 (bottom), 12 (top), 13,
   15 (top), 16, 37 (top)
Bes Stock: 1, 3 (center), 27, 34, 39 (bottom)
Victor Englebert: 3 (bottom), 21, 22, 23, 24,
   25, 26, 33, 35, 36, 37 (bottom), 41, 43
Ayesha C. Ercelawn: 29 (bottom), 45
Focus Team — Italy: 7
HBL Network Photo Agency: 6, 15
   (center and bottom), 18 (bottom)
The Hutchison Library: 14 (bottom)
Earl Kowall: 20
North Wind Picture Archives: 10, 11
Christine Osborne Pictures: 39 (top), 40
Philippine Department of Tourism —
   Singapore Office: 2, 8, 9 (top), 31
Pietro Scòzzari: 12 (bottom), 32, 38
Topham Picturepoint: 3 (top), 4, 19,
   29 (top), 30
Travel Ink Photo and Feature Library: 17
Trip Photo Library: Cover, 14 (top), 28

Digital Scanning by Superskill Graphics Pte Ltd

Contents

Words that appear in the glossary are printed in **boldface** type the first time they occur in the text.

4

Welcome to the Philippines!

The Philippines is known as the *Pearl of the Orient Seas*. This **archipelago** of 7,107 islands is a land of volcanoes, gulfs, lakes, and waterfalls. Once a United States colony, the Philippines became independent in July 1946. Let's visit the Philippines and its people.

Opposite: Many Filipinos live near the fertile slopes of volcanoes such as Mount Isarog on the island of Luzon.

Below: Children are considered a blessing from God in this mainly Catholic nation.

The Flag of the Philippines

The current Philippine flag combines the designs of past flags. The white stands for equality, the blue for unity and peace, and the red for courage and loyalty. The three stars represent main regions. The sun rays represent provinces that fought Spain.

The Land

The Philippines lies between Taiwan to the north and Borneo and the islands of Indonesia to the south. Covering 115,830 square miles (300,000 square kilometers), it is bigger than the United Kingdom but smaller than Japan. With so many islands, the Philippines has the world's longest broken coastline, at 22,549 miles (36,281 km). Only 880 of the islands are **inhabited**.

Below:
The coastline of the Philippines has many beautiful bays and beaches like this one on the island of Bohol.

The country has seven mountain ranges. The Cordillera Central and the Sierra Madre, both located on the island of Luzon, are the largest. At 9,692 feet (2,954 meters), Mount Apo, on the island of Mindanao, is the country's highest peak.

Among the natural wonders of the Philippines are Luzon's Pagsanjan Falls and Lake Taal, a crater lake with an active volcano in the center of it.

Above: The 1,776 uniformly shaped Chocolate Hills on Bohol Island are a rare natural land formation. Filipino legend says that these hills are the tears of a giant who lost his love.

Climate

The Philippines has a hot and humid climate with two seasons. The dry season lasts from December to May, and the wet season is from June to November. Each year, monsoon winds blow from the northeast between November and April and from the southwest between May and October.

Left: Lake Taal's plants and animals feel the constant tremors of the active Taal Volcano. Their habitat also has fierce storms called typhoons. About fifteen of these storms hit the islands each year with strong winds and heavy rains that cause a lot of damage.

Left: About fifty different types of bananas grow in the Philippines.

Plants and Animals

A wide variety of plants and animals thrive in the Philippines. Fruits such as mangoes, chicos, and durians grow well in the tropical sunshine. Animals such as monkeys, jungle fowl, deer, and hornbills live in the forests. The many kinds of fish and **crustaceans** in the waters include the world's largest fish, the whale shark, and one of the smallest, the dwarf pygmy.

Below: This parrot shares its home on Palawan Island with giraffes, zebras, and impalas that were shipped from Africa to the Philippines in 1977 so they would not be harmed in a civil war.

History

The islands of the Philippines are over a million years old, but the Negritos were probably the first humans to live there, only about twenty-two thousand years ago. They were later joined by settlers from Malaya and Indonesia. With traders from China, India, and the Middle East, the country became a melting pot of cultures.

Victoria.

Left: Portuguese navigator Ferdinand Magellan was the first European to set foot on the Philippines. This drawing shows his ships being welcomed at Mactan near Cebu. It also shows Filipinos and Spaniards in battle.

In 1521, Ferdinand Magellan, while leading a Spanish expedition, explored the archipelago. It was later named "the Philippines" for Spain's King Philip II. Spain established a permanent **settlement** on the island of Cebu in 1565. Although the Spanish united all of the islands under a central government in Manila and introduced Christianity to the Filipinos, they also mistreated the natives. In 1896, the Filipinos attempted a **revolution**.

Above:
This painting shows Magellan being killed by Lapu-Lapu, a fierce local chief.

An American Colony

In mid 1898, the Philippines declared independence from Spain. That year, the Spanish-American War began, and the Filipinos fought on the side of the Americans. They hoped that, after the war, the United States would respect their independence, but in December 1898, the Philippines became a U.S. colony. The Americans improved government and education, but the Philippines was not yet independent.

The Japanese Occupation

When the Japanese bombed Pearl Harbor in December 1941, the United States declared war on Japan. The two nations battled over the Philippines, which was the U.S. colony closest to Japan. In 1942, Japan took over the Philippines, but the United States regained control in 1945. On July 4, 1946, the United States granted the Philippines independence.

Below: U.S. general Douglas MacArthur led the mission to end Japanese control of the Philippines.

The Marcos Years

Filipinos enjoyed **democracy** for twenty-six years. Democracy ended, however, in September 1972, when President Ferdinand Marcos took control of the country as a dictator. Marcos was forced out by the People Power Revolution in February 1986.

Above: Ferdinand Marcos and his wife, Imelda, led a very extravagant lifestyle from 1966 to 1986, when Marcos was in power.

Left: On the way to Baguio, tourists pass this sculpture of Marcos carved on Mount Sto Tomas along the Marcos Highway.

Maria Corazon Aquino (1933–)

Maria Corazon Aquino was the first female president of the Republic of the Philippines. In 1986, she won an election against Marcos. When he refused to hand over power, Aquino organized the non-violent People Power Revolution to remove him.

Maria Corazon Aquino

Fidel Valdez Ramos (1928–)

In spite of a close friendship with Ferdinand Marcos, Fidel Valdez Ramos supported Aquino during the 1986 revolution and became chief of staff in her government. He was elected president in 1992. The Philippine economy improved greatly while he was in office.

Fidel Valdez Ramos

Joseph Ejercito Estrada (1937–)

Joseph Estrada was an actor before he was elected president in 1998. In January 2001, he was arrested for **corruption**. Gloria Arroyo, his vice-president, then became president.

Joseph Ejercito Estrada

Government and the Economy

After the Marcos **regime** ended, new leaders of the Philippines **enacted** a **constitution** that limits the elected president to only one six-year term.

Below: Malacañang Palace is both the home and office of the president. It is located in Manila.

The president is assisted by an elected vice-president and an appointed cabinet. The Philippine government also has a congress with a twenty-four-member Senate and a House of Representatives that can have up to 250 members.

In 1991, the Philippine government transferred many responsibilities to the local government units (LGUs) in the provinces, cities, and *barangays* (bar-RUNG-guys), or villages. LGUs help create organizations to improve education and public health. They also

help build community spirit by getting the citizens involved in public meetings and projects. The Philippine army is an important part of the government, too, helping out in both times of peace and times of disaster.

Above: Like many of the government buildings in the Philippines, the Philippine Congress Building in Manila looks very much like a government building in the United States.

Natural Resources

The Philippines is rich in marine life, forests, minerals, and energy sources. Coastal waters provide pearl oysters, seaweed, and sponges, while forests **yield** bamboo, rattan, and many other building materials. In addition to large reserves of **geothermal** energy and natural gas, the Philippines has many mineral **deposits**. Gold and copper are common on Luzon. Iron, nickel, and marble are found on other islands.

Above: Fish are sorted for export at the Manila Harbor fish port.

Below: Philippine pearls are some of the largest pearls in the world.

Agriculture and Industry

Many Filipinos work in agriculture. Among the crops they grow are rice, corn, sugar, sweet potatoes, fruits, and tobacco. The country's fruits are sold all over Asia. The Philippines is also the world's biggest producer of coconuts and **hemp** items, and it is the second biggest producer of sugar. Although it also produces food, cloth, and medicine, the Philippines imports more of these products than it exports.

Below: A worker at the Larpanday Banana Plantation on Mindanao checks the quality of the fruit before it is exported.

People and Lifestyle

Most Filipinos are descendants of native Negritos and peoples who came from Malaysia and Indonesia. The country's major **ethnic groups** include the Visayans, the Tagalogs, and the Ilocanos. Other Filipinos are a variety of ethnic minorities. About half of them are Muslims. Some are *mestizos* (mis-TEE-sohs), who have a mixed ancestry of either Spanish or Chinese and Filipino.

Below: These women are from the Ifugao tribe, an ethnic minority in the Philippines. The Ifugaos live in the mountainous areas of the north.

Filipinos can be divided into the rich, the middle class, and the poor. The rich are a small group but have 85 percent of the country's wealth. Most of them are mestizo landowners or businessmen. Professionals, such as doctors, lawyers, engineers, and architects, belong to the middle class. The rest of the population is extremely poor. Approximately 30 percent of Filipinos live below the **poverty line**.

The Family

Families are important in Filipino culture. Many Filipinos either live in **extended families** or spend a lot of time with family members.

Most Filipinos think of children as gifts from God. Some parents try to have a say even in their children's adult lives. Children are expected to respect and obey their parents for as long as they live.

Above: This just-married couple is leaving a church in Manila. Because most Filipinos are Roman Catholics, they usually get married in a church.

Values

Filipinos have many positive values, such as a respect for **authority** and a high regard for the dignity of all people. They are grateful for favors and believe in repaying them. Their respect for authority comes from a traditional respect for older family members. Unfortunately, this attitude sometimes discourages independent thinking and has given the people in authority a great deal of power.

Below: This Filipino family is enjoying a picnic lunch at the Rizal Park in Manila.

Education

Filipino children attend six years of elementary school and four years of high school. Elementary education is free. Classes are taught in Pilipino and English, the country's official languages. Until 1987, Spanish was also required. Today, students can choose to study many other languages and dialects, even Mandarin Chinese. The literacy rate in the Philippines is the third highest in Asia.

Below: More than 90 percent of all elementary students in the Philippines attend government schools such as this one in Davao.

Philippine schools are run either by the government or by private groups. The private schools are very costly, so almost all elementary and about two-thirds of all high school students enroll in government schools.

Private universities are usually run by religious groups. The University of Santo Tomas, founded by Spanish Dominican priests in 1611, is the oldest university in the Philippines.

Above: The statues of nine Philippine saints stand in front of the library of the University of Santo Tomas in Manila.

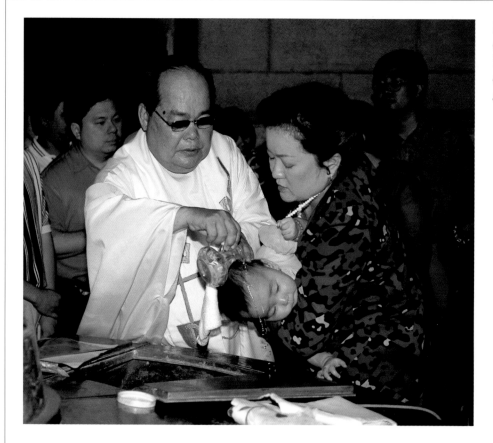

Religion

Most early Filipinos were **animistic** and worshiped **ancestral** spirits known as *anitos* (ah-NEE-tohs). They believed these spirits lived in rivers, fields, old trees, and mountains. The Spanish introduced Christianity to the country in the 1500s. Today, most Filipinos are Roman Catholics. Other Filipinos are Protestants, Muslims, Buddhists, or members of smaller religious groups.

Pagan Beliefs

The Philippines is the only country in Asia with mainly Christian people and where **pagan** beliefs are still strong. Many Filipinos believe in witches, or *mangkukulam* (MUNG-koo-koo-lum), ghosts, or *multo* (mool-TOH), and **voodoo**, or *kulam* (KOO-lum). Some of them also have faith in the power of amulets, charms, and love potions. A magical herb called *odom* (OH-dohm) is believed to make a person invisible.

Below: Quiapo mosque is one of the places where Filipino Muslims go to pray. About 5 percent of the Filipino population are Muslims.

Language

Filipinos speak English, which is one of their official languages, and over one hundred different native languages and dialects. Pilipino, their other official language, came from Tagalog, one of the eight main native languages.

Storytelling and Literature

Ancient Philippine **folklore** was passed from one generation to the next through storytelling. Famous **epics** include the Ifugao people's *Hudhud and Alim.*

Left: Philippine newspapers, books, and magazines are published in many different languages, including English.

Left: A monument to Dr. José P. Rizal in Manila honors his literary and political work.

The writer Dr. José P. Rizal is the national hero of the Philippines. In his book *Noli Me Tangere*, or *Touch Me Not*, he blamed the Spanish for the country's problems. Rizal's writings have inspired patriotism among the Filipinos. He was executed in 1896 for helping a rebellion against Spain.

Above: Rizal's books criticized Spanish rule.

Arts

Theater

In the 1800s, moro-moro and zarzuela were popular Philippine theater styles. Moro-moro plays were about conflict between Christians and Muslims, while zarzuela was a kind of **satirical** opera. Movies are now more popular than plays in the country, yet Lea Salonga, a Philippine stage perfomer, is well-known as Kim in *Miss Saigon*.

Below: Bayanihan dancers are famous for their skillful folk dancing. Here they perform outside the Malacañang Palace in Manila.

Architecture

Early houses in the Philippines were made of nipa, bamboo, and other native woods. Called *bahay kubo* (BAH-hay koo-BOH), these houses were raised 10 to 16 feet (3 to 5 m) above ground for better **ventilation**. Between the sixteenth and the nineteenth centuries, Spanish Baroque architecture was popular. Then came Antillean houses, which were made entirely of wood.

Above: Baroque-style architecture is seen in the old buildings of some Philippine cities.

Dance and Music

Philippine dances have Malay and Spanish influences, yet they are uniquely Philippine. For example, La Jota Manilena is Manila's version of La Jota Moncadena, a dance that combines Spanish and Ilocano steps, accompanied by bamboo castanets.

Philippine music is even more **indigenous** than its dances. It uses native instruments such as a *kudyapi* (kood-JAH-pee), a two-stringed lute.

Above: Singing and dancing play important roles in Philippine culture.

Crafts

Every Philippine region produces a special type of craft, such as textiles or baskets. *Piña* (PEEN-yah) is one kind of handwoven cloth used to make the *barong tagalog* (BAH-rong tah-GAH-lawg), the national shirt of Filipino men. Basket designs vary by region. On Mindanao, they are made of black nito vine. The Ifugaos on Luzon use smoke-stained materials.

Below: A woman from Panay sews intricate designs on piña, which is cloth woven from pineapple fibers.

Leisure

Each month brings a new celebration in the Philippines. The country's **fiestas** feature street parades, fireworks, and beauty pageants, and Filipinos love them. Catholic festivals started when the country was under Spanish rule, but they have since become distinctly Philippine festivals and include native beliefs and practices.

Below: Music lovers in Manila often enjoy free concerts in Rizal Park on weekends.

Entertainment

Families in the Philippines often go shopping together on weekends. Filipinos also like to go see crafts at open-air bazaars. Going to movies and watching television are also favorite pastimes. Although the country has its own movies and television programs, many Filipinos prefer American soap operas and miniseries. Not everyone can afford a TV set, so some people go to a neighbor's home to watch.

Above: Philippine theaters show a variety of movies, both local and imported from other countries.

Sports

Introduced by Americans, basketball is one of the most popular sports in the country. Philippine professionals and amateurs play throughout the year, and competitions are held in every region.

The Philippines has produced many world-class athletes in sports such as boxing, golf, and bowling. Filipino bowler Paeng Nepomuceno has won four Bowling World Cups.

Above: Villagers watch as young Filipinos play a basketball game. Almost every Philippine village has at least one basketball court.

Jai alai (HIGH-lye), a version of handball, is a popular spectator sport. It is a fast game played indoors with a ball and a cesta, or crescent-shaped wicker basket, instead of a racket.

Sipa (SEE-pah) is another spectator sport. In it, players must keep a hollow rattan ball in the air by kicking it with their knees, legs, and feet. In *palo sebo* (PAH-loh SEE-boh), a traditional fiesta sport, players climb a greased bamboo pole for a cash prize at the top.

Above: In jai alai, the ball is hit against the high walls around the court.

Below: Crowds in Mindanao gather to watch amateur boxing matches.

Festivals

Since most Filipinos are Roman Catholics, many religious festivals revolve around Christian holidays. Christmas and Lent are celebrated widely. Holy Week, the last week of Lent, is a solemn time during which the country almost comes to a stop. At this time, television programs are mostly religious, and some Filipinos frown upon loud music.

The *Ati-Atihan* (ah-TEE-AH-tee-hun) is a three-day event held every year, during the third week of January, in the city of Kalibo. This festival celebrates the arrival, in 1212, of four Bornean *datus* (DAH-toos), or chiefs, who bought Panay from the Aetas. Kalibo's town square is colorfully decorated for the festival, and dance rituals are performed daily. A holy mass on the last day is followed by a four-hour procession of local tribes.

Above: An ethnic minority, known as the Igorots, or "people from the mountains," live in Cordillera Central.

Left: At Ati-Atihan, festival goers often paint their faces and dress up like thirteenth-century native peoples. The different ethnic groups wear colors and patterns that distinguish them from each other.

Food

Malay, Spanish, Chinese, American, Arab, and Indian cultures influence cooking in the Philippines. Meals are traditionally eaten with the fingers, but modern Filipinos prefer utensils. A typical meal is meat or fish with vegetables and rice, which is often eaten three times a day. Many meals include a sauce made of vinegar, hot chili or soy sauce, and lime juice.

Below: Filipinos often invite visitors for dinner. In their culture, dinner is the most important meal of the day.

Pork crackling, or *chicharon* (TSEE-tsah-rone), and marinated raw fish, or *kinilaw* (kee-nee-LAW), are popular Philippine appetizers. *Adobo* (AH-doh-boh), which is made with chicken or pork cooked in vinegar, soy sauce, garlic, and spices, is sometimes called the national dish. Most feasts include *lechon* (LEHR-tsone), or suckling pig stuffed with spices and roasted until the skin is crisp and the meat is tender.

Above: This food stall in a Manila shopping center sells traditional cooked food.

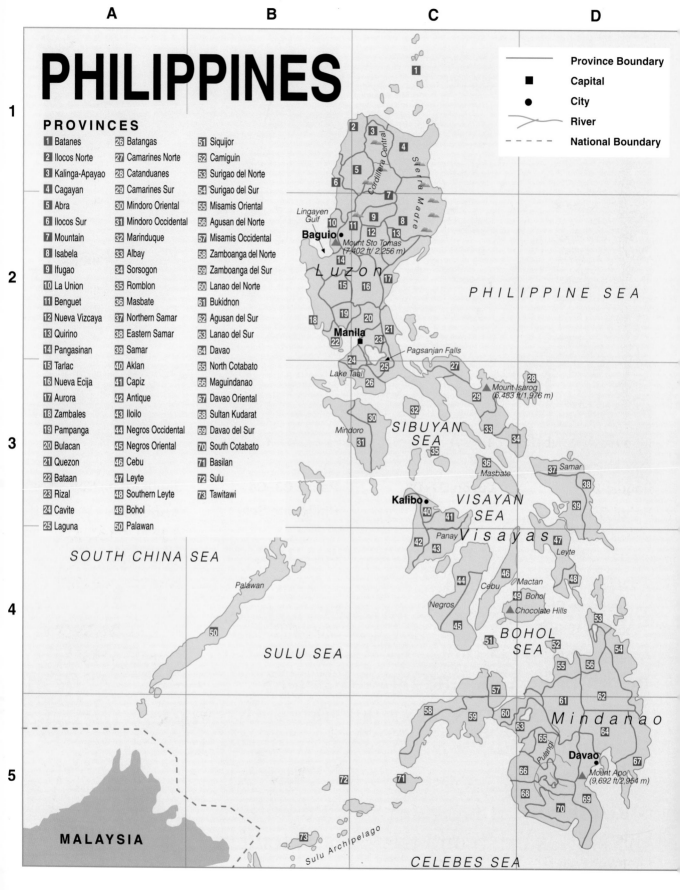

PHILIPPINES

PROVINCES

1 Batanes	**26** Batangas	**51** Siquijor
2 Ilocos Norte	**27** Camarines Norte	**52** Camiguin
3 Kalinga-Apayao	**28** Catanduanes	**53** Surigao del Norte
4 Cagayan	**29** Camarines Sur	**54** Surigao del Sur
5 Abra	**30** Mindoro Oriental	**55** Misamis Oriental
6 Ilocos Sur	**31** Mindoro Occidental	**56** Agusan del Norte
7 Mountain	**32** Marinduque	**57** Misamis Occidental
8 Isabela	**33** Albay	**58** Zamboanga del Norte
9 Ifugao	**34** Sorsogon	**59** Zamboanga del Sur
10 La Union	**35** Romblon	**60** Lanao del Norte
11 Benguet	**36** Masbate	**61** Bukidnon
12 Nueva Vizcaya	**37** Northern Samar	**62** Agusan del Sur
13 Quirino	**38** Eastern Samar	**63** Lanao del Sur
14 Pangasinan	**39** Samar	**64** Davao
15 Tarlac	**40** Aklan	**65** North Cotabato
16 Nueva Ecija	**41** Capiz	**66** Maguindanao
17 Aurora	**42** Antique	**67** Davao Oriental
18 Zambales	**43** Iloilo	**68** Sultan Kudarat
19 Pampanga	**44** Negros Occidental	**69** Davao del Sur
20 Bulacan	**45** Negros Oriental	**70** South Cotabato
21 Quezon	**46** Cebu	**71** Basilan
22 Bataan	**47** Leyte	**72** Sulu
23 Rizal	**48** Southern Leyte	**73** Tawitawi
24 Cavite	**49** Bohol	
25 Laguna	**50** Palawan	

Legend:
- Province Boundary
- ■ Capital
- ● City
- River
- National Boundary

Above: Pedicabs, a traditional form of transportation, are popular on Leyte.

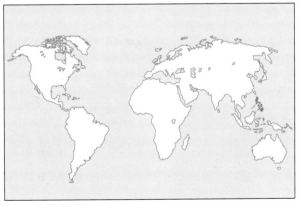

Quick Facts

Official Name	Republic of the Philippines
Capital	Manila
Official Languages	Pilipino and English
Population	81,841,518 (2001 estimate)
Land Area	115,830 square miles (300,000 square km)
Coastline	22,549 miles (36,281 km)
Largest Island	Luzon 40,420 square miles (104,688 square km)
Main Island Groups	North: Luzon, Mindoro, Palawan
	Visayas: Bohol, Cebu, Leyte, Masbate, Negros, Panay, Samar
	South: Mindanao
Major Mountains	Cordillera Central, Sierra Madre
Highest Point	Mount Apo 9,692 feet (2,954 m)
Longest River	Pulangi River 200 miles (320 km)
Main Ethnic Groups	Ilocanos, Tagalogs, Visayans
Major Religion	Roman Catholicism
Currency	Philippine Peso (51.35 PHP = U.S. $1 as of 2001)

Opposite: Jeepney owners take pride in keeping their vehicles clean and colorful.

Glossary

ancestral: relating to earlier generations of family members.

animistic: believing that every part of nature has a spirit or a soul.

archipelago: a group of many islands.

authority: people with the knowledge or power to enforce laws or standards.

constitution: a set of the basic laws used to govern a country.

corruption: the dishonest use of power or position for personal gain.

crustaceans: kinds of hard-shelled animals, including lobsters and crabs, that live in water.

democracy: a system of government in which citizens elect the officials who govern the country.

deposits: masses of materials that build up by natural processes.

enacted: made into a law.

epics: long poems that tell the story of a historical or legendary hero.

ethnic groups: groups of people who share a certain race or culture.

extended families: family groups that include close relatives.

fiestas: festivals or celebrations.

folklore: stories, customs, and beliefs passed down through generations.

geothermal: related to heat energy from within Earth.

hemp: a plant with fibers in its stalk that are used to make rope and strong cloth.

indigenous: of a particular area.

inhabited: lived on by people.

pagan: having little or no religion or worshiping more than one god.

poverty line: the minimum income to meet basic needs, such as food, clothing, and housing.

regime: the time during which the government of a certain leader is in power.

revolution: a conflict to bring about a change in government.

satirical: criticizing people or ideas by using humor to show their faults.

settlement: a new community or village started by a small group of people.

ventilation: the flow of fresh air.

voodoo: a type of magic or witchcraft believed to harm people by pricking a figure or a toy that represents them.

yield: produce, especially by growing.

More Books to Read

Abadeha: The Philippine Cinderella.
    Myrna J. de la Paz (Shen's Books)

Christmas in the Philippines. Cheryl
    L. Enderlein (Bridgestone Books)

Multicultural Folktales for All Ages.
    Vincent M. Kituku and Felisa G.
    Tyler (Vincent Muli Wa Kituku)

The People of the Philippines.
    Celebrating the Peoples and
    Civilizations of Southeast
    Asia series. Dolly Brittan
    (Powerkids Press)

Philippines. Festivals of the World
    series. Lunita Mendoza
    (Gareth Stevens)

Philippines. Globe-Trotters Club
    series. Anne E. Schraff
    (Carolrhoda Books)

The Philippines. Countries of the
    World series. Lucile Davis
    (Bridgestone Books)

The Philippines. Enchantment of the
    World series. Walter Oleksy
    (Children's Press)

Rockabye Crocodile: A Folktale from
    the Philippines. Jose Aruego
    (Econo-Clad Books)

Tales from the 7,000 Isles: Popular
    Philippine Folktales. Artemio
    R. Guillermo (Vision Books)

Videos

Philippines Travel Preview series.
    (Education 2000)

The Philippines: Pearls of the Pacific.
    (Library Video)

Web Sites

sim.soe.umich.edu/parol

www.folklife.si.edu/festival98/
    phil98.htm

www.fotw.stm.it/flags/ph.html

www.kgma.org

Due to the dynamic nature of the Internet, some web sites stay current longer than others. To find additional web sites, use a reliable search engine with one or more of the following keywords to help you locate information about the Philippines. Keywords: *Corazon Aquino, barong tagalog, Filipino, Luzon, Manila, Philippines.*

Index